The Ultimate Questions Book ~ Life

Copyright © 2013 Marketing Tao, LLC. All rights reserved. No part of this material shall be used for any purpose other than intended. Nor shall any part of this product or the materials included be reproduced by any means, including electronically stored, without the written permission of Kathy Jo Slusher and Marketing Tao, LLC.

Table of Contents

Skillful Questioner 2
Making Questions Powerful 7
How to Use This Book 9
Additional Uses 11
Open and Closed-Ended Questions Chart 14
General Life Coaching Questions 15
Life Wheel 45
Professional Development Questions 46
Family Questions 48
Personal Development Questions 50
Spirituality Questions 52
Finances Questions 54
Health & Wellness Questions 56
Relationships Questions 58
Fun & Enjoyment Questions 60
Life Values / Quality Assessment 62
Blank Wheel 64
Life Quotes 65
SMART Goals Checklist 70
About the Work 71
About the Authors 72
Additional Resources 73

The Skillful Questioner

Problems cannot be solved by the same level of thinking that created them.
    ~ Albert Einstein

During the Renaissance there was a massive resurgence of learning and a gradual yet widespread shift in education, leading to economic growth and development, political and social reform, and an increase in trade and commerce.

The Industrial Revolution was a major turning point in human history. There were immense technological advancements, economic progress, income & population growth, and an increase in the standard of living never seen before.

Why?

They were asking themselves powerful questions that shifted the way they approached problems, and spurred curiosity and creativity.

Today, we are on the verge of another major shift. To make the leap we need to make we must ask ourselves and our clients questions that achieve & surpass that same level of curiosity and creativity.

The quality of questions we ask directly influence the knowledge we acquire and the actions we take.

By asking quality, empowering questions we can find the answers leading to the change we seek.

Being a skillful questioner is more than just the words used in the questions. It's as much about how you ask the questions as it is about the words you use. Having no attachment to the outcome of the question and addressing the questioner with curiosity, objectivity and in a non-confrontational manner creates an atmosphere of safety for the questionee to answer honestly and thoroughly.

The Ultimate Questions Book ~ Life

With over 30 years of coaching, training, facilitation, and experiential learning experience between the two of them, both Denny & Kathy Jo recognize even the most skilled professionals can sometimes get stuck finding the right questions.

Asking powerful questions allow the questionee to see things differently, open up creativity, gain new perspectives, see solutions, discover their own answers, deepens relationships and trust, and improves problem-solving and decision-making abilities.

You can ask the most empowering questions and unlock amazing possibilities, but unless you truly listen and the questionee feels that intent, forward movement is stunted. Listening is an important part of communication as is asking powerful questions. However, not all listening is effective listening.

It is said that hearing is a physical ability. We all hear. We don't always listen. Listening is a skill, one that must be practiced and intentional to be effective.

As a vital part of the questioning process, listening enables:
- The acquisition of new information
- Greater insight to the values, strengths, behavior and needs of the questionee
- The questionee to discover his / her own perspectives of the situation
- Trust & Rapport
- Understanding of underlying meaning
- Motivation
- Depth & Intimacy
- Mutual understanding
- The questionee to feel heard and understood

Levels of Listening

There are 4 Levels of Listening. We have all experienced listening to others and being listened to at each level. The higher the level the more energy is required to maintain that level. Not every conversation you have will take place at the Intuitive Listening level.

1. **Competitive Listening**: The main focus in Competitive Listening is on the listener's own thoughts. Here the listener is more interested in their own views and is waiting for an opportunity to jump in and react.

2. **Attentive Listening**: The main focus in Attentive Listening is on the words being said. There is genuine interest in hearing and understanding what is being said but assumes an understanding, not checking with the questionee for confirmation.

3. **Reflective Listening**: The main focus in Reflective Listening is on a deeper and clarified understanding of what is being said. There is genuine interest in listening, not just hearing, as well as understanding what is being said and confirms that understanding, often through mirroring back the exact information shared.

4. **Intuitive Listening**: The main focus in Intuitive Listening is an understanding of the meaning behind what is said. There is genuine desire to understand not only the meaning of what is being said but also the tone, pitch, speed, of what's being said, the body language that accompanies the words, what is being said behind the words, and what is NOT being said.

We all know how important communication is. However, the vast majority of communication isn't spoken. According to studies done in the '70s by Albert Mehrabian, only 7% of communication takes place through exchange of words. The remaining 93% of information is communicated through body language, eye contact, and pitch, speed, tone and volume of the voice.

Understanding that most information is not communicated through words, to be a powerful listener there are several things you have to keep in mind while listening to the questionee.

The Ultimate Questions Book ~ Life

Keys to Powerful Listening

1. Intentions are set to gain a greater understanding of the questionee, their behavior, thinking, values, beliefs, perspectives and needs.
2. Stay Curious.
3. Detached Involvement: the ability to tap into deep levels of empathy and place yourself in the questionees position, understanding their thoughts and feelings without taking on their emotions.
4. Focus on what is being communicated in all areas – body language, tone, pace, pitch, energy – while not focusing on your response.
5. Offer feedback and request clarification if necessary.
6. Remember silence is golden. Don't be afraid of silence. Allow the questionee to sit with the question and ponder.
7. Use Intuitive Listening as much as possible.

When entering a conversation where you are required to deeply listen and understand questionees, try your best to enter the situation with as much energy as possible.

Powerful Questions + Intuitive Listening + Acknowledgement + Time to Respond = Unlocked Potential & Possibilities

Making Questions Powerful

Asking the right questions in the right way is key to achieving the right results. Powerful questions immediately access our creative, holistic brain from which solutions are born. These thought provoking questions are designed to forward your client's actions through clarifying, inspiring, probing, challenging, affirming, exploring, opening new possibilities, connecting, assessing, and evaluating, leading to the right solutions for your client.

When crafting questions, there are 3 things you must consider.
1. The Scope of the Question
2. The Construction of the Question
3. Assumptions & Bias in the Question

Scope

The Scope is defined as the range or subject matter that something deals with or to which it is relevant. The scope covers the domain of inquiry. Matching the scope of the question to meet the needs of inquiry increases the capacity to effect change and sets the questionee up for success. Therefore, keep within realistic boundaries of the situation and questionee's knowledge and power.

For example: "How can you best change your perspective?" as opposed to "How can you change the perspective within the organization?"

When determining the scope of your question you must first determine the scope of the answer you are seeking. If you are looking for greater clarification you must ask questions designed to gain clarity. If you are looking for greater insight, you must ask questions designed to go deeper. If you are looking at obstacles you must ask questions designed to uncover blocks. The scope of the answer determines the category of the question to achieve an appropriate response. You can find the question categories under the General Questions section of this book.

The Ultimate Questions Book ~ Life

Construction

The construction of a question consists of the language, intention and tone you take when asking the question. A question's construction is a critical element in either opening up one's mind to possibilities or closing the mind to solutions. The construction of a question can determine the depth and direction of the answers. Are you looking for a direct yes or no answer? Ask a closed-ended question. Are you looking for deeper clarification? Do you want to open choices or create a new picture? Ask open-ended questions.

The construction of a question stimulates reflective thinking and deepens the conversation. Starting your question with either "who" or "how" determines the level and direction of inquiry. For example: "Who can help you to make this happen?" "How can this happen?"

When constructing the question, ask yourself what "work" you want this question to do.

Assumptions and Bias

Part of being human is that our experiences and perspectives influence the way we think. We all carry with us assumptions and biases. We cannot eliminate them. Awareness of assumptions and biases allow us to be on the look-out for them as we construct and ask our questions, and listen to the answer.

One of the most commonly used questions containing an assumption or bias is "What is wrong?" This question assumes a negative.

Reframing is a potent way to reword questions freeing them of assumptions and bias such as from "What's wrong?" to "What happened?" Reframing encourages deeper reflection and shifts assumptions into possibilities for creating forward action.

A Word About "Why"

Some of the most powerful questions begin with "Why." Some of the most dangerous questions begin with "Why." Why-questions can lead to greater insight and more thorough answers.

The Ultimate Questions Book ~ Life

They ask the questionee to go deeper and evaluate. Answers to why-questions speak about the inner feelings, beliefs, and motives of the questionee. Because of the highly personal nature of why-questions, safety and trust must be established in the relationship. If not, a why-question can easily trigger reactive behaviors and blame detracting from solutions.

The difference between getting greater insight and triggering reaction is the level of safety the questionee feels in the relationship and the way in which the question is asked.

If safety and trust have been established on both sides of the relationship and a why-question is the most appropriate question to ask, stay curious when asking your question. This will keep the non-verbal elements of asking a question as well as your intention on maintaining safety and trust and away from blame.

Choose why-questions carefully and sparingly.

Characteristics of a Powerful Question

1. Solutions-focused
2. Clear & Simple
3. Involves Values & Ideals
4. Generates Curiosity
5. Stimulates Reflection
6. Thought-Provoking
7. Engages Attention
8. Focused
9. Touches Deeper Meaning
10. Leads to More Questions

How to Use This Book

As you encounter a specific challenge in your life or your client's life, you may become stuck and not know where to go next. This book is designed to assist in getting unstuck by sparking new, unique, and in-depth questions. You can either use these questions as is or allow them to inspire new ideas for you.

Open / Closed-Ended Questions Chart: Open-Ended questions are designed to require the answerer to go deeper and give more detail. These types of questions should be used as often as possible to gain greater detail, inquiry, and increase understanding. Closed-Ended questions are excellent for commitment. These are used ONLY when looking for a "yes" or "no" response.

General Life Questions: These general Life questions are a great starting point for coaching around Life issues. These questions are designed around a basic coaching approach of: clarifying, creating a vision, defining choice, identifying blocks and barriers, evaluating, prioritizing, probing, and scaling. Use these questions as touch-stones throughout the process. Categorized based on your client's specific needs and situation, these questions increase the scope of the coaching relationship.

Life Wheel: The Life Wheel is a self-awareness assessment you can use for yourself or your client to rate the level of satisfaction in each area of the Life Wheel. Use the Wheel to broaden the scope of coaching to encompass each area to create the ideal Life.

Wheel Specific Questions: As your partnership deepens and gaps in Life skills present themselves, you can target different areas of Life more in-depth through these questions. Use Wheel Specific questions to prolong the coaching partnership and develop a more purposeful life.

Life Values / Qualities Assessment: Rate Life Values / Qualities by how important they are to you and how much you walk your talk can help you identify where gaps may be in your client's Life Skills. This is an excellent resource in identifying areas and opportunities for growth.

Blank Wheel: Using the Blank Wheel, fill in your or your client's top 8 Life Values / Qualities and rank these to address the gaps of creating their ideal Life. You can also develop new coaching assignments and opportunities around each area.

Life Quotes: This collection of Life Quotes is a great resource for either your own marketing efforts or to deepen the level of thinking for your clients. Use these quotes to send inspirational emails, add to your website, use as topics for your newsletters or to Tweet.

SMART Goals Checklist: SMART Goals help ensure success. Goals that are unattainable or unreasonable are a direct line to failure. Failure stifles excitement, passion, and commitment. To ensure the success of your clients, check each goal against the SMART Goals checklist to determine how viable the goal truly is and keep your client's on track.

The Ultimate Questions Book ~ Life

Additional Uses for This Book

Coaching/Consulting Role

→ Use the Life Wheel Assessment in a Complementary Session

→ Assess a client's level of satisfaction in the 8 key areas of the Life Wheel in an introductory session to establish the partnership foundation

→ Use SMART Goals checklist as an evaluation & progression tool

→ Create accountability around the SMART Goals checklist

→ Identify strengths & gaps in each area of the Life Wheel

→ Identify initial coaching goals

→ Use the questions as preparation for coaching sessions

→ Create customized assignments using the questions

→ Create visualizations & meditations based around the Life Wheel segments or Questions

→ Use quotes in sessions to stimulate fresh perspectives

→ Add quotes to client emails for inspiration

→ Create a customized assignment by journaling on quotes

→ Create a mastermind or group discussion around a specific quote

→ Help clients set goals using the SMART Goals checklist

Product & Services Development

→ Use this book and the Life Wheel as your Signature Program

→ Use Life Wheel Assessment in a workshop as an assessment or discussion tool

→ Add the Life Wheel Assessment to your current Signature Program or product

→ Use questions as an idea generator

→ Create an E-course / E-book / E-workbook series around segments of the Life Wheel

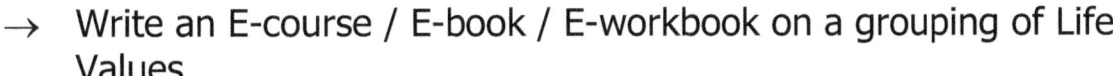

→ Develop workshops & seminars around segments of the Life Wheel

→ Form Mastermind Groups around key Wheel segments

→ Use Life Values / Qualities list as an idea generator

→ Write an E-course / E-book / E-workbook on a grouping of Life Values

→ Create Workshops & Seminars on a grouping of Life Values

→ Add a quote to a product or presentation for inspiration or point emphasis

→ Use quote in workshop as a discussion topic

→ Use SMART Goals checklist in a workshop as tool to move participants forward

Marketing / Business Development

→ Use the Life Wheel Assessment as a prospect pre-qualifier

→ Create a prequalifying survey for prospects with questions

→ Use questions or quotes in ezine / newsletter

→ Post a question / quote to your target audience on a LinkedIn Discussion

→ Use a series of questions to outline a promotional teleclass

→ Create a free download of questions around a particular topic

→ Use questions in Blog & Twitter Posts

→ Write an article based on the questions

→ Write an article based on an individual Life Value

→ Use the Life Values Assessment as a pre-coaching prep form

→ Create an ezine / newsletter around individual Value

→ Post a quote on your blog / Facebook / LinkedIn asking for comments about how it relates to the topic

→ Use a quote to inspire a podcast or video

→ Use quote to motivate an article idea

→ Post Quote on Blog / Twitter

Open-Ended vs. Closed-Ended Questions

Open-Ended questions invite others to discuss in detail what is important to them. They are used to gather information, establish rapport, and increase understanding. These questions do not lead and are not geared towards expected outcomes. When used, the asker must be willing to listen and respond appropriately.

Closed-Ended questions are used to elicit a definitive yes or no answer. Use only when you want a definite yes or no. They are particularly useful when gaining a commitment.

Ask Open-Ended questions whenever possible.

Open-Ended Questions Start with:	Closed-Ended Questions Start with:
Who	Is
What	Does
How	Are
Why	Do
When	Will
Where	Can

General Life Coaching Questions

Clarifying

Clarifying questions are designed to lay the groundwork and foundation for attaining goals. They set the stage, remove ambiguity, elicit details, and supply known facts.

Ask Clarifying Questions when you need a clear picture of where the questionee is currently at, what resources are available, what perspectives they have, as well as ant a picture of where the questionee is coming from, what they want, and the reality of the situation.

Ask these questions as a starting point, to establish a framework.

Example of Clarifying Questions

Questionee: I want to feel more freedom in my life.

Questioner: What do you mean by more freedom?

Questionee: I mean to have the ability to do what I want when I want to.

Questioner: Give me an example.

The Ultimate Questions Book ~ Life

Clarifying Questions

- Who has made an impact on your life?
- On whom do you depend?
- Who depends on you?
- Who encompasses your inner circle?
- Who do you most appreciate?
- Who supports you?
- Who comes first in your life?
- Who brings you the most joy?

- Who do you need to consider?
- To whom do you need to express that?
- With whom do you need to set stronger boundaries?
- What does that represent to you?
- Considering this new information, what would you like to do?
- What feelings does that bring up?
- What areas of your life does that affect?
- What are your gifts?
- What are your core values?
- What inspires you?
- Where can you improve your skills?
- Where do you find joy?
- When have you used that in the past?

The Ultimate Questions Book ~ Life

- → When have you been successful?
- → When have you failed?
- → When have you been let down in the past?
- → When was the last time you just let go?
- → When do you put yourself first?
- → When was the first time you took control?
- → Why is that important to you?
- → Why would that make a difference?
- → Why do you seek clarity around this?
- → Why are you here?
- → Why is that important to you?
- → Why does this need to change?
- → Why do you need to let this go?
- → How did you do that?
- → How did that work for you?
- → How does that stop you?
- → How does that inspire you?
- → How can you use this information to your best advantage?
- → How has that worked in the past?
- → If you had it just the way you wanted it, how would that feel?
- → How would that make a difference?
- → How do you express yourself?
- → How do you define happiness?

Visioning

Visioning questions are designed to establish a desired end result. These questions create a picture of the future so a plan on how to get there can be created.

Visioning Questions allow the questionee to "see" the result they are working to achieve. This opens possibilities, engages creativity, and keeps motivation high and direction clear.

Ask Visioning Questions when creating a new reality, establishing an end-result, identifying the ideal, or giving direction to move forward.

Example of Visioning Questions

Questioner: What would you ideally like to see happen?

Questionee: I would like to move to the country away from the noise and congestion of the city. I would like to grow my own food, and live more simply. I would like to see the stars at night and hear the crickets sing.

Questioner: In this ideal vision, what do you see yourself doing?

Questionee: I see myself writing that book I keep talking about and having time to putter around in my flower garden.

Questioner: How would you feel if you had that?

Questionee: I see myself really happy, living a good life with the people I love, enjoying the things that give my life meaning.

Questioner: That is a beautiful picture for you.

Questionee: Yes it is!

The Ultimate Questions Book ~ Life

Visioning Questions

- → Who shares your vision?
- → Who would you most like to become?
- → Who would you become if you knew you could not fail?
- → Who supports your grand vision?
- → Who do you need support from to realize this vision for your life?
- → Who do you become when truly inspired?
- → What would you prefer to have in your life?

- → What does the ideal life look like to you?
- → What is your ideal image of ___?
- → What will it take to manifest your dream?
- → What is the grandest vision you have for your life?
- → Where will that make a difference?
- → Where else can you do that?

The Ultimate Questions Book ~ Life

- → If money were no object, where would you go / live / spend your time?
- → Where would you like to be?
- → Where do you want to be this time next year, in 5 years, in 10 years?
- → When have you experienced success / happiness / joy / peace?
- → When do you need to be clear on your intentions?
- → When do you need to gain clarity before you speak?
- → Why is this vision important to you?
- → Why do you want to create a new vision for your life?
- → Why would you let that person stop you from realizing your vision?
- → How would you like to live?
- → How well does your life fit into your image of the ideal life?
- → How can you fill the gaps between your ideal life image and where you are currently at?
- → How often do you dream of a better life?
- → How would realizing your dream change your life?

The Ultimate Questions Book ~ Life

Choice

Choice Questions are meant to show options, empower, and accept responsibility. These questions lend to out-of-the-box thinking and demonstrate options and opportunities.

Ask Choice Questions when questionee feels trapped, hopeless, or feels as though there is no other answer, and needs a new perspective & empowerment to move forward.

Example of Choice Questions

Questionee: I don't know what to do. I really would like to attend that seminar next Saturday and Sunday but my husband wants to take the kids to the cabin that same weekend. We always do everything together.

Questioner: If you knew no-one would be upset, what options do you have to resolve this?

Questionee: You mean, if I went to the seminar and my husband took the boys to the cabin without me?

Questioner: What would happen if that could be the reality?

Questionee: Well that certainly would be different.   Maybe that would work. I will talk with my husband tonight.

Choice Questions

- Who ultimately makes that decision?
- Who can you ask for help?
- Who can help you make the right choice?
- Who helps you decide?
- Who tries to interfere with your decisions?
- Who could you turn to gain the clarity you desire?
- Who do you choose?
- What decision do you need to make?
- What are your choices?
- What would you like to do?
- If you knew no one would be hurt by your choice, what would you choose?
- What do you need to let go of to make that happen?
- What decision does your ideal life need you to make today?
- What would you do differently?
- What would you never, ever do?
- Where else do you want to feel that way?
- Where would you like to go?
- Where have you avoided making a decision?

The Ultimate Questions Book ~ Life

- → Where could you make a different choice that would help you more?
- → When is the best time to decide?
- → When do you need to make this decision?
- → When would it be too late?
- → When do you trust your gut in making decisions?
- → When have you regretted not listening to your gut?
- → Why are you hesitating?
- → Why not do it today?
- → Why would you make that choice knowing what you know?
- → Why are you listening to everyone else except yourself?
- → How will you make that decision?
- → How could that choice help you?
- → How could that choice hurt you?
- → How often do you make the right choice?
- → How can your intuition help guide you here?

The Ultimate Questions Book ~ Life

Blocks & Barriers

These questions are designed to uncover & examine what is stopping the questionee from moving forward, seeing progress, and gaining what they truly want.

Ask Blocks and Barrier Questions when you sense hesitation, resistance, goal hopping, or a belief they are unable to move forward.

Example of Blocks & Barriers Questions

Questionee: I really would like to date again but can't seem to put myself out there.

Questioner: What do you think is getting in the way?

Questionee: I'm not sure…..maybe my fear.

Questioner: Fear of what?

Questionee: Fear of not being attractive enough….of no one being interested in me.

Questioner: So you would rather stay home alone where it is safe than risk getting rejected again.

Questionee: As pitiful as that sounds, yes, I think that is it.

Questioner: How well will that work for you?

Questionee: Not very well at all since I want to meet someone! I guess we have some more work to do!

Questioner: I guess we do!

The Ultimate Questions Book ~ Life

Blocks & Barriers Questions

- → Who gets in your way?
- → Who stops you dead in your tracks?
- → Who can help you overcome this block?
- → Who knows the way around this obstacle?
- → Who throws roadblocks in your path?
- → Who has the biggest influence in keeping you stuck?

- → Who could you become if this obstacle was no longer in your way?
- → Who limited you as a child?
- → Who helped you overcome challenges in the past?
- → Who is standing in your way?
- → What stops you?
- → What do you need to push past? To go around?
- → What do you need to get over this hump?
- → What thoughts or feelings get in the way of you achieving ___?
- → What limiting belief do you have around _____?
- → What judgments are you placing on yourself?
- → What judgments do you carry about that?
- → What is the biggest challenge in your life?
- → What motivates you through tough times?

The Ultimate Questions Book ~ Life

- → What internal / external blocks do you have that hold you back from your ideal life?
- → What makes that challenge particularly difficult?
- → What is the hardest thing you have ever done?
- → What obstacles have you overcome in your life?
- → What masks are you wearing on a daily basis?
- → Where do you find it the most challenging to be authentic?
- → Where do you limit yourself?
- → Where do you need to improve your life skills?
- → Where is your biggest stumbling block?
- → When are you in fight, flight, or freeze?
- → When do you feel least empowered?

- → When in your life is it the most difficult to put yourself first?
- → When do you feel the most locked down?
- → When do you experience doubts the most?
- → When was the last time you felt truly free?
- → Why wear that mask any longer?
- → How does wearing that mask serve you?
- → How can you shift your beliefs about your life to better serve you?
- → How does your image of how life should be mask your true feelings?

Evaluating

Evaluating Questions determine criteria. They evaluate or estimate the nature, quality, extent or significance of situations. They assess factors such as needs, issues, processes, performance, and outcomes. They can also determine the pros & cons of a situation.

Ask Evaluating Questions when the questionee needs to establish a clearer sense of their wants and needs related to a particular situation.

Example of Evaluating Questions

Questionee: I want to achieve more success at work.

Questioner: What would that look like?

Questionee: I would work more efficiently and get things done on time.

Questioner: What would be different if you were more efficient?

Questionee: I would lead meetings with more confidence and get more buy-in from the team.

Questioner: How would it feel if you achieved all of that?

Questionee: Great!

The Ultimate Questions Book ~ Life

Evaluating Questions

→ Who would you most like to meet? Why?

→ With whom would you most like to spend time? Why?

→ Who could give you the best support with that?

→ To whom do you offer your best?

→ To whom would you most like to give your time?

→ What have you done before in this situation?

→ What was successful about that?

→ What was less than successful about that?

→ What is the most daring thing you have done?

→ What do you need to do to take the best advantage of this situation?

→ Where have you been at your best?

→ Where do you feel most peaceful / alive / passionate / excited / calm / balanced / comfortable / in your element?

→ Where is your favorite place in the world?

→ Where do you need to have more passion in your life?

→ Where are you most appreciated?

→ When was the last time you expressed your true self?

→ When do you feel most powerful?

→ When do you feel most secure?

The Ultimate Questions Book ~ Life

- → When do you feel the most vulnerable?
- → When does that come up the most?
- → When have you experienced the deepest sense of who you are?
- → Why is happiness / joy / success / freedom / peace / fulfillment important?
- → Why does being authentic matter to you?
- → Why do you feel pressed to make a change now?
- → Why is that direction best for you at this time?
- → Why is that least important to you?
- → Why is that most important to you?
- → How important is it to be happy?
- → How do you measure happiness?
- → How strong are your life skills?
- → How important is peace / joy / success / happiness / freedom / fulfillment to you?
- → Without them saying a word, how can to tell someone is at peace / joyful / successful / happy / free / fulfilled?
- → How do you know when your life is falling short?
- → How do you know when it excels?

The Ultimate Questions Book ~ Life

Goal Setting

Goal Setting Questions are designed to move into and forward the action. They include aspects of accountability, step-by-step action, and an understanding of what needs to be done in order to accomplish the desired goal(s).

Goal Setting Questions are intended to set the questionee up for success. In order to accomplish this there are certain factors to be considered when designing a goal plan.

SMART Goals help construct a format for creating successful goals.

Ask Goal Setting Questions when the questionee is ready to move into action.

Example of Goal Setting Questions

Questionee: I decided I want to return to college and finish my degree.

Questioner: That's great! When would you like to begin?

Questionee: Next semester but I have some things I need to do first.

Questioner: What do you see as the 1st step to take to get started?

Questionee: Well, I need to talk with an admissions counselor and figure out what credits will transfer and how many credits I need to complete my degree. Then I have to decide which classes to start with.

Questioner: That sounds like a plan. When will you make the appointment?

Questionee: This week. I am excited!
    (Move onto creating SMART Goals *pg 70)

Goal Setting Questions

- Who can help you with that?
- With whom do you need to connect to get started?
- Who could help hold you accountable?
- Who could easily accomplish what you are trying to achieve?
- Who do you need to be in order to accomplish that?
- What steps can you take right now?
- What is 1 thing you can do to move you forward?
- What have you always wanted to do?
- What are your top three goals right now?
- What would you most like to accomplish?
- What areas of your life need more attention?
- What are you (not) willing to do?
- What can be done to realize that dream?
- What have you accomplished so far?
- What is waiting to be accomplished?
- What would you like to get done this week?
- What would you like to get done this month?
- What would you like to complete within a year?
- What 3-5 things do you absolutely want to do before you die?

The Ultimate Questions Book ~ Life

- → Where would you like to go with this?
- → Where do you want to spend more time?
- → Where in your life do you feel unsatisfied?
- → Where could you give that more attention?
- → When do you want this to happen?
- → When do you need to get started?
- → When do you want to start?
- → When you implement these changes into your life, how will things be different?
- → Why are you committed to doing this?
- → How can you implement that into your life?
- → How can you recreate that again?

Prioritizing

Prioritizing Questions identifies and weighs importance, values and benefits. They can also be used to rank & order.

Prioritizing Questions are great to use in conjunction with Goal Setting Questions and can also help reduce overwhelm.

Ask Prioritizing Questions when the questionee needs to put their priorities in order or examine what is important to them.

Example of Prioritizing Questions

Questionee: I have so many things I need to get done. I feel overwhelmed!

Questioner: That is understandable considering all you have on your plate. Let's make a list of everything you have to do.

Questionee: OK.

(Together they create a list of to-do's)

Questionee: That's a lot! No wonder I feel overwhelmed.

Questioner: I hear you! Let's chunk it down. Of these 12 items, which are the most urgent and necessary to get done this week?

Questionee: I would have to say numbers 3, 6 and 7. The others can wait. I feel much better.

The Ultimate Questions Book ~ Life

Prioritizing Questions

- → Who are your priorities?
- → Who needs to me more of a priority in your life?
- → Who is the most important person in your life?
- → Of what do you need to do more?
- → Of what do you need to do less?
- → What are the top 3-5 must-haves in your life?
- → What place should consciousness have your life?
- → What would a highly conscious life entail?
- → What should a highly conscious life avoid?
- → What are your current priorities?
- → What additional priorities are weighing on you?
- → What is your number one priority?
- → What can you do to make that more of a priority?
- → What is your main concern?
- → What seems inconsequential?
- → What really matters to you?
- → What doesn't matter?
- → What does that say about your priorities?
- → What is the most crucial thing your life needs right now?
- → Where are your priorities perfectly aligned?
- → Where are your priorities in conflict?

The Ultimate Questions Book ~ Life

- → Where are your priorities out of whack?
- → Where have you been able to prioritize effectively in the past?
- → Where do your priorities and values align?
- → Where do your priorities and values clash?
- → When will you give that the time it needs?
- → When have you made that a priority in the past?
- → When can you find the time for that?
- → When does that become the most vital goal?
- → When will you begin to focus on that important objective?
- → When have you managed your priorities the best?
- → When do your priorities get jumbled?
- → Why are these priorities the most important?
- → Why not rearrange your priorities?
- → Why are clear priorities important for you?
- → Why do your priorities help you stay on track?
- → Why have you not made that your number one priority before now?
- → Why should you place yourself at the top of your list?
- → How would making yourself your number one priority change your life?
- → How often do you focus just on yourself?
- → How would having those three priorities make a difference?

The Ultimate Questions Book ~ Life

Probing

Probing Questions make the questionee go deeper, drawing out more details, concerns, challenges, knowledge, and issues about a particular situation. A good Probing Question requires thought. These questions are used to get out the root of the situation, and reveal thoughts, feelings, and details under the surface.

Ask Probing Questions when going deeper into an issue or concern will bring greater insight and help uncover new awareness; thoughts and feelings lying below the surface.

Example of Probing Questions

Questionee: I really don't want to do my presentation tomorrow.

Questioner: Why not?

Questionee: I don't know. Even though I put a lot of time into preparing it, I guess I don't think it's very good. I'd rather hold off until I can make it better.

Questioner: From what you described last time, it appears you have a solid presentation.

Questionee: Yeah, I guess so. I just itself aside, what are you really worried about?

Questionee: (Pause) That I will freeze…nothing will come out of my mouth and look like a bumbling fool!

Questioner: That is quite a worry.

Questionee: I didn't realize how anxious I am about speaking to the group.

Questioner: How would it be for us to work on that together?

Questionee: Yes, please! That would be great.

The Ultimate Questions Book ~ Life

Probing Questions

- Who do you admire?
- Who did you always want to be when you were a child?
- Who would you be if you lived an authentic life?
- Who are you allowing to take away your energy / authenticity / power?
- Who drains you?
- Who feeds your soul?
- Who takes you for granted?
- Who stifles your creativity / truth / self-expression?
- With whom do you need to share your true feelings?
- What if that were true?
- What difference would that make?
- What is in your control?
- What is in the control of others?
- What is the real answer we're looking for?
- What need does that serve?
- What's the deeper thought?
- What are your thoughts around _____?
- What action results from that thought?
- What feeling does that thought create?
- What is the deeper meaning to that?

- → What is the real issue?
- → What would you rather think about?
- → What is not being said?
- → What is missing in your life?
- → What would it take to have the life you want?
- → What beliefs do you have around your role in life?

- → What affect do these beliefs have on your life?
- → If you were in your advanced years and had an opportunity to tell a fresh-out-of-college young adult the most important thing you learned in your life, what would you tell them?
- → If you had to describe your life in just three words, what would you say?
- → What beliefs do you have around how you should live your life?
- → What is more important in your life, living from the head or the heart?
- → If someone lived purely from the head, what would that look like?
- → If someone lived purely from the heart, what would that look like?
- → What would a combination of the two look like?
- → Where does that sit in your body?
- → Where do you feel the most accepted?
- → Where do you feel judged?
- → Where else do you need to access that feeling?

The Ultimate Questions Book ~ Life

- → Where does that work for you?
- → Where does that work against you?
- → Where do you feel inspired / adventurous / stifled / free / confined?
- → When was the last time you were truly happy with your life?
- → When is it important to live to the fullest?
- → When is your life smooth?
- → When is your life rough?
- → When you think of _____, what feelings come up for you?
- → Where do you feel the most authentic?
- → Why should your life change?
- → Why must you be strong?
- → Why are your boundaries being crossed?
- → How does that thought serve you?

- → How comfortable are you with living life to the fullest?
- → How much do your thoughts affect your happiness?
- → How can you shift these thoughts to better serve you?
- → How do you relate to these feelings?

New Perspectives

New Perspective Questions are designed to shift the direction of thinking. By shifting thinking the questionee can shift the way they approach the world and situations. These questions often create "aha" moments as they elicit options and possibilities previously not considered.

Ask New Perspective Questions when the questionee persists in levels of thinking that include anger, blame, victim, trapped or when they are unable / unwilling to see alternatives.

Example of New Perspective Questions

Questionee: I think my sister is upset with me.

Questioner: What makes you think that?

Questionee: Because she hasn't returned my calls this week.

Questioner: How certain are you she is upset with you?

Questionee: Well, why else wouldn't she call me back?

Questioner: Great question! What might be some other reasons she hasn't called you back yet?

Questionee: Well, maybe she's really busy with work. I know she had a big project she was working on and her boss can set some tough deadlines. I bet that's it.

The Ultimate Questions Book ~ Life

New Perspective Questions

→ Who would you like to be?

→ Who would you like to be / become through this process?

→ Who would you become if fear was no longer your regular companion?

→ Who would you become if joy was your middle name?

→ What would you change about your life if you could?

→ If you could have it just the way you want it, what would that look like?

→ If you were to use a geometric shape to describe your life, what shape would you chose and why?

→ What is another way to think about that?

→ If you were to describe your life as a weather pattern, what would it be?

→ What haven't you thought of yet?

→ What would be the most courageous thing you could do today?

→ What skills could you draw on to make that happen?

→ When you look at yourself in the mirror, what do you see?

→ What would you do if you knew you could not fail?

→ Where can you make the biggest difference?

→ Where does that thought take you?

→ Where would you like to see your life lead you?

→ Where can you carve out more space for you?

Marketing Tao , LLC

The Ultimate Questions Book ~ Life

- → Where might you find the support you need?
- → Where is your place in the world?
- → When is your life a straight line / curve / spiral?
- → When does life feel worth living?
- → When was the best time in your life?
- → When are you the proudest?
- → When are you filled with joy?
- → When do you feel at peace?
- → Why would looking at this differently help you?
- → Why should you look at that differently?
- → Why should you let go of that thought?
- → Why not give life a chance?
- → Why live a half-life?
- → How do you inspire & motivate others?
- → How special are you?
- → How special do you feel?

- → How often do you congratulate yourself?
- → How can you celebrate your success?
- → How will you be remembered?
- → How would you like to be remembered?
- → How could you bring more excitement to life?
- → How would loving life more help you?
- → How might you begin showing deep appreciation for all that you have?

The Ultimate Questions Book ~ Life

Scaling

Scaling Questions help gauge and determine the level of concern, commitment, and importance. They are a tool that identifies where the questionee would position themselves, the situation or determining a level. Scaling Questions can be used to help measure progress, attitude and behavioral change, and situational shifts.

Ask Scaling Questions when the questionee wants to gauge the level of concern, commitment, or importance of a situation or concern.

Example of Scaling Questions

Questioner: On a scale of 1-10, 1 being not at all and 10 being extremely, how important is that for you?

Questionee: I would say about an 8.5.

Questioner: That's pretty important!

Questionee: Yes, it really is.

Marketing Tao, LLC

Scaling Question

- → On a Scale of 1 to 10, (10 = couldn't be happier and 1 = not happy at all) where would you rank yourself? Why did you rank yourself that way?

- → On a Scale of 1 to 10, (10 = completely and 1 = not at all) how well do your beliefs of yourself work for you? Why did you rank yourself that way?

- → On a Scale of 1 to 10, (10 = completely and 1 = not at all) how comfortable are you in your life? Why did you rank yourself that way?

- → On a Scale of 1 to 10, (10 = completely and 1 = not at all) how satisfied are you in your life? Why did you rank yourself that way?

- → On a Scale of 1 to 10, (10 = enormous and 1 = none) how much joy is in your life? Why did you rank yourself that way?

- → On a Scale of 1 to 10, (10 = extremely and 1 = not at all) how committed are you to turning your life around? Why did you rank yourself that way?

- → On a Scale of 1 to 10, (10 = extremely and 1 = not at all) how comfortable are you with digging deep to uncover what's really interfering with your happiness? Why did you rank yourself that way?

- → On a Scale of 1 to 10, (10 = extremely and 1 = not at all) how ready are you to accept responsibility of your life? Why did you rank yourself that way?

- → On a Scale of 1 to 10, (10 = extremely and 1 = not at all) how comfortable are you with the idea of letting go? Why did you rank yourself that way?

- → On a Scale of 1 to 10, (10 = extremely and 1 = not at all) how ready are you to start transforming your life right now? Why did you rank yourself that way?

Life Wheel

The Ultimate Questions Book ~ Life

Directions: for each section of the Life Wheel, circle the number that represents your current level of satisfaction in that area. The higher the number, the greater your level of satisfaction.

LIFE

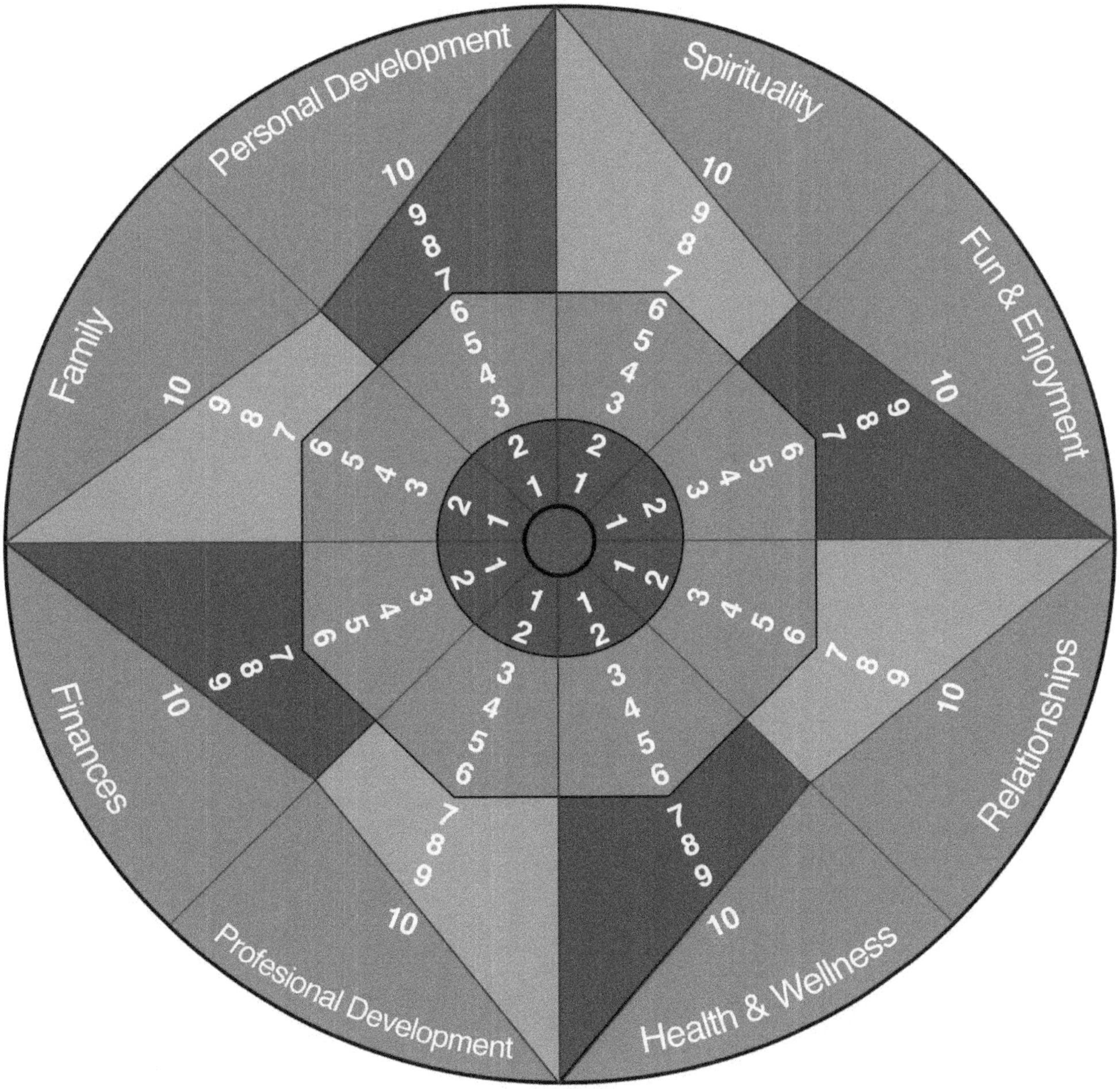

Sections: Personal Development, Spirituality, Fun & Enjoyment, Relationships, Health & Wellness, Profesional Development, Finances, Family

© 2013 Unaltered Reproduction Rights Granted, Marketing Tao, LLC

The Ultimate Questions Book ~ Life

Professional Development

Who

- Who would you prefer to be seen as at work?
- Who are you in relation to your job?
- With whom do you experience the most challenges at work?
- With whom do you enjoy working?
- Who can help you get your foot in the door?

What

- If money was no object and you could do whatever you wanted, what would you do?
- What does success mean to you?
- What is the downside?
- What three qualities describe what you do at work?
- What could you do to be happier at work?

Where

- Where would you prefer to work?
- Where are you the most skilled?
- Where can you improve your skills?
- Where do you excel at work?
- Where do you find passion in your career?

The Ultimate Questions Book ~ Life

When

- → When are you satisfied at work?
- → When are you less than satisfied at work?
- → When do you need to plan for a change?
- → When do you express yourself at work?
- → When are you appreciated at work?

Why

- → Why is it important to be happy with your career?
- → Why is success important to you?
- → Why is it important to work / stay at home / change profession?
- → Why did you enter this profession when you first started?
- → Why does / doesn't it work for you now?

How

- → How would you prefer to feel at work?
- → How would changing your job benefit you?
- → How can you think differently about your job?
- → How does your job serve you right now?
- → How would your life be different if you loved what you did for a living?

Your Questions on Career & Profession

- → _____
- → _____
- → _____
- → _____

The Ultimate Questions Book ~ Life

Family

Who

→ Who do you need to be as a parent?

→ Whose needs do you place above your own?

→ With whom do you need to communicate more?

→ With whom do you need to communicate less?

→ Who benefits the most from effective communication?

What

→ What needs to happen to increase the connection with your family?

→ What serves as a warning sign that you are losing control?

→ What 3 qualities would you use to describe your family / ideal family?

→ What are your beliefs about parenting / child-rearing?

→ What is your parenting style?

Where

→ Where have setting boundaries with your family served you?

→ Where are you consistent / inconsistent?

→ Where does your attention need to be focused?

→ Where do you need to gain more control?

→ Where do you compromise?

Marketing Tao, LLC

The Ultimate Questions Book ~ Life

When

- → When is the right time to listen?
- → When is the right time to speak?
- → When are you the happiest with your family?
- → When are you able to truly be yourself with your family?
- → When do you need a break from your family?

Why

- → Why is effective communication important in parenting?
- → Why do you feel the need to work on your relationship / parenting skills?
- → Why do you think this is happening now?
- → Why do you need boundaries with your family?
- → Why do you sacrifice for your family?

How

- → How does your family support you?
- → How much time do you allocate for self-care?
- → How much time is ideal to spend with your family?
- → How would you describe your ideal family?
- → How do you spend your time with your family?

Your Questions on Family

- → _____
- → _____
- → _____
- → _____

The Ultimate Questions Book ~ Life

Personal Development

Who

- → Who is your authentic self?
- → Who defines you?
- → Who brings out the best in you?
- → Who has been the most influential person in your life?
- → Who do you reach out to for advice / support?

What

- → What strategies do you need to employ to continue with your personal growth?
- → What needs to happen for you to take control of your life?
- → What needs to happen to let go of the need for control over your life?
- → What has been your journey thus far?
- → What needs to happen for you to break through this block?

Where

- → Where do you feel the most connected?
- → Where do you love to spend your time?
- → Where do you need to develop yourself further?
- → Where are your attentions diverted?
- → Where do you need to slow down?

Marketing Tao, LLC

The Ultimate Questions Book ~ Life

When

- → When are you growing / learning?
- → When do you feel stagnant?
- → When do you need to be stagnant?
- → When do shine?
- → When do you feel deflated?

Why

- → Why is personal development important to you?
- → Why are you unsatisfied with where you are at?
- → Why make this choice over that one?
- → Why is continual growth important?
- → Why is it important to pace yourself?

How

- → How do you learn best?
- → How are you different when you feel you're growing?
- → How can you utilize the resources you currently have available to achieve you goals?
- → How can you maintain balance?
- → How important is personal development to you?

Your Questions on Personal Development

- → _____
- → _____
- → _____
- → _____

The Ultimate Questions Book ~ Life

Spirituality

Who

- → Who is responsible for your ideas of spirituality?
- → Who are you really?
- → Who do you want to be?
- → Who brings out the best in you?
- → With whom do you want to connect more on a spiritual basis?

What

- → What does it mean to be spiritual?
- → What creates barriers to engaging in spiritual endeavors?
- → What can you do to be more spiritual?
- → What opportunities for spiritual growth do you experience every day?
- → What would a spiritual life look like to you?

Where

- → Where do you resist listening to your wise inner voice?
- → Where do you need to be more spiritually disciplined?
- → Where do you experience doubt or lack of faith?
- → Where do you find peace?
- → Where can your sense of intuitive knowing help you?

The Ultimate Questions Book ~ Life

When

- → When are you afraid to look at your inner self?
- → When are you confident?
- → When do you feel the most connected?
- → When do you feel disjointed?
- → When is spirituality important?

Why

- → Why is spirituality important to you?
- → Why is spiritual development essential?
- → Why do you have a spiritual practice?
- → Why do you need a sense of greater knowing?
- → Why is nurturing your spiritual nature vital?

How

- → How can you develop a deeper spiritual connection?
- → How willing are you to commit to spiritual practice?
- → How can you use your spiritual connection to move forward?
- → How much time do you want to devote to your spiritual development?
- → How does being spiritually centered make your life easier?

Your Questions on Spirituality

- → _____
- → _____
- → _____
- → _____
- → _____

The Ultimate Questions Book ~ Life

Finances

Who
- Who are you in relation to money?
- Who influenced your beliefs around money?
- Who taught you how to handle money?
- Who defined the value of money for you?
- Who do you have to become to face your money issues?

What
- What is your greatest challenge with money?
- What thoughts come up for you when thinking of money?
- What beliefs influence your thoughts about money?
- What do you believe you deserve?
- What do you need to let go of, move through, face or resist in order to address this challenge?

Where
- Where do you avoid money?
- Where does money cause the greatest challenges for you?
- Where do you need to face your money challenges head on?
- Where might you be stressed, frustrated, or worried?
- Where might it serve you to let go of stress, frustration, or worry?

When
- When do you ignore, deny, or hide from money challenges?
- When do you fight when confronted with money challenges?

The Ultimate Questions Book ~ Life

→ When does money energize you?

→ When do you see challenges?

→ When do you see solutions?

Why

→ Why is financial health important to you?

→ Why do you want to solve this money issue?

→ Why would balancing your budget help you?

→ Why do you avoid money issues?

→ Why is money scary?

How

→ How do your beliefs about money get in your way?

→ How does money serve you best?

→ How much time do you spend worrying about money issues?

→ How can you let go of your fears / worries of money?

→ How many things do you worry about that are not worth worrying about?

Your Questions on Finances

→ _____

→ _____

→ _____

→ _____

→ _____

→ _____

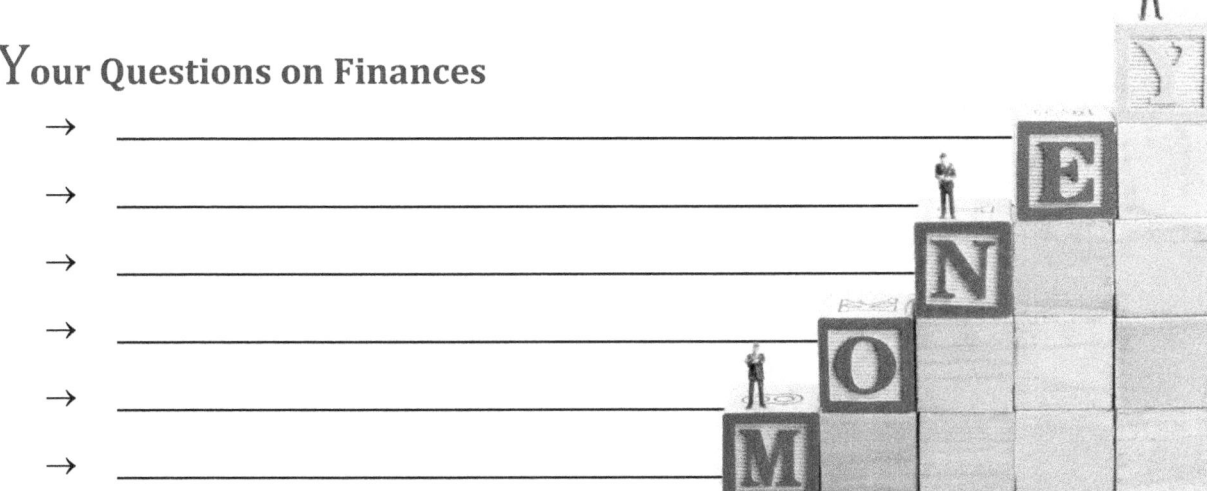

Health & Wellness

Who

- → Who are you under-utilizing when it comes to maintaining your health?
- → Who are you in relation to your physical being (your body)?
- → Who influences your choices about your health & wellness?
- → Who can become your best ally?
- → Whose choice is it?

What

- → What resources do you need to live a healthy life?
- → What grounds you?
- → What is the difference between health & wellness to you?
- → What does it look like to be healthy?
- → What would be different for you if you did lead a healthy lifestyle?

Where

- → Where can you be healthier?
- → Where do you enjoy exercising?
- → Where would the ideal place be for you to enjoy meditating / exercising / walking / nature / etc.?
- → Where is your greatest physical / emotional strength?
- → Where have you cultivated a healthy lifestyle?

When

→ When do you need help most?

→ When do you need help least?

→ When do you feel healthy?

→ When do you feel unhealthy?

→ When do you feel at your best?

Why

→ Why is balance important?

→ Why is being healthy important?

→ Why do you feel you need to bring more wellness into your life?

→ Why have you not maintained a healthy lifestyle?

→ Why do you deny yourself permission to be healthy?

How

→ How does your health affect your life?

→ How does your health define who you are?

→ How can you bring more wellness into your life?

→ How open are you to trying new things?

→ How do you feel about pushing yourself beyond your limits?

Your Questions on Health & Wellness

→ _____

→ _____

→ _____

→ _____

→ _____

Relationships

The Ultimate Questions Book ~ Life

Who

→ Who sets you off? Why?

→ Who calms you down? Why?

→ Who makes you feel small or insignificant? Why?

→ Who shows compassion towards you? Why?

→ Who makes you feel on top of the world? Why?

What

→ What makes a good friend / husband / daughter etc?

→ What do you need out of this relationship?

→ What is important about understanding how your emotions affect those around you?

→ What are your beliefs about what a marriage / friendship / parent – child relationship should look like?

→ What impacts this relationship the most?

Where

→ Where do you feel like yourself the most in this relationship?

→ Where are you stifled?

→ Where have you avoided telling the truth?

→ Where have you spoken from the heart?

→ Where would you like this relationship to be 3 years from now?

Marketing Tao, LLC

The Ultimate Questions Book ~ Life

When

- → When does this relationship nurture you and feed your soul?
- → When are you most supported?
- → When are you the least supported?
- → When do you need more?
- → When do you need less?

Why

- → Why is understanding how you feel important in this relationship?
- → Why have you avoided your feelings in the past?
- → Why are feelings helpful?
- → Why is it important to be authentic in this relationship?
- → Why does this relationship need to change?

How

- → How comfortable are you sharing your true feelings?
- → How can you create an atmosphere of safety for this other person to share their true feelings?
- → How can you be a better partner / friend / sister / father / etc?
- → How do emotions guide your choices?
- → How can you give more?

Your Questions on Relationships

- → _____
- → _____
- → _____
- → _____

The Ultimate Questions Book ~ Life

Fun & Enjoyment

Who

→ With whom do you like to hang out?

→ With whom do you have the most fun?

→ Who do you admire most?

→ Who brings out the kid in you?

→ Who is like-minded?

What

→ What do you do for fun?

→ What brings you the most joy?

→ What makes you smile?

→ In what way does adventure play a part in your everyday life?

→ What would you like your life look like if it was an action adventure movie?

Where

→ Where do you need more adventure?

→ Where do your plans to have fun break down?

→ Where do you need to be more / less serious?

→ Where should people always enjoy themselves?

→ Where do you enjoy yourself the most?

The Ultimate Questions Book ~ Life

When
- → When do you need fun the most?
- → When is your most enjoyable time of the day?
- → When does fun come knocking at your door?
- → When has your life been the most enjoyable?
- → When, in the day, are you at your best?

Why
- → Why is there no time for fun?
- → Why is fun frivolous?
- → Why (not) take a risk?
- → Why does your life need more fun?
- → Why does having fun allow you to be more productive?

How
- → How many times do you laugh in a day?
- → How can you have more fun?
- → How do you have fun?
- → How can you laugh like you did when you were young again?

Your Questions on Fun & Enjoyment
- → _____
- → _____
- → _____
- → _____
- → _____

Life Values/Qualities Assessment

Directions: Identify your top 8 Life Values / Qualities. How closely do you live these Values / Qualities?

- ☐ Abundance
- ☐ Acceptance
- ☐ Accountability
- ☐ Achievement
- ☐ Adaptability
- ☐ Adventure
- ☐ Ambition
- ☐ Appreciation
- ☐ Assertive
- ☐ Authenticity
- ☐ Awareness
- ☐ Balance
- ☐ Beauty
- ☐ Boldness
- ☐ Candor
- ☐ Celebration
- ☐ Character
- ☐ Charismatic
- ☐ Comfortable with Change
- ☐ Commitment
- ☐ Communication Skills
- ☐ Community Development
- ☐ Competency
- ☐ Consciousness
- ☐ Cooperative
- ☐ Courage
- ☐ Creativity
- ☐ Critical Thinking Skills
- ☐ Decisiveness
- ☐ Dedication
- ☐ Delight
- ☐ Dependability
- ☐ Disciplined
- ☐ Diversifier
- ☐ Driven
- ☐ Education
- ☐ Empathy
- ☐ Endurance
- ☐ Enthusiasm
- ☐ Emotional Intelligence
- ☐ Energetic
- ☐ Enthusiastic
- ☐ Ethical
- ☐ Excitement
- ☐ Face Adversity
- ☐ Fairness
- ☐ Family
- ☐ Flexibility
- ☐ Focused
- ☐ Follow-Through
- ☐ Forward Thinking
- ☐ Freedom
- ☐ Fun
- ☐ Goal-Oriented
- ☐ Gratitude
- ☐ Grounded
- ☐ Harmony
- ☐ Healthy Relationships

© 2013 Unaltered Reproduction Rights Granted, Marketing Tao, LLC

The Ultimate Questions Book ~ Life

- ☐ High Expectations
- ☐ High Standards
- ☐ Humility
- ☐ Humor
- ☐ Holistic Thinking
- ☐ Honesty
- ☐ Innovative
- ☐ Inspiration
- ☐ Interdependent
- ☐ Integrity
- ☐ Interpersonal Skills
- ☐ Intuition
- ☐ Joy
- ☐ Justice
- ☐ Learner
- ☐ Level-Headed
- ☐ Listener
- ☐ Love
- ☐ Loyalty
- ☐ Mature
- ☐ Motivation
- ☐ Nature
- ☐ Non-judgment
- ☐ Objectivity
- ☐ Openness
- ☐ Opportunistic
- ☐ Optimistic
- ☐ Ownership of Actions
- ☐ Passion
- ☐ Patience
- ☐ Persuasive
- ☐ Playfulness
- ☐ Pro-Active

- ☐ Productivity
- ☐ Purpose
- ☐ Respectful
- ☐ Responsibility
- ☐ Risk Taking
- ☐ Rule-Breaker
- ☐ Rule-Oriented
- ☐ Self-Awareness
- ☐ Self-Care
- ☐ Self-Esteem
- ☐ Self-Growth
- ☐ Self-Less
- ☐ Self-Regulation
- ☐ Service-Oriented
- ☐ Simplicity
- ☐ Solutions Focused
- ☐ Spirituality
- ☐ Spontaneity
- ☐ Straightforward
- ☐ Strength
- ☐ Structured
- ☐ Supportive
- ☐ Tactful
- ☐ Tenderness
- ☐ Tolerance
- ☐ Tough
- ☐ Trust
- ☐ Truthfulness
- ☐ Understanding
- ☐ Values-Oriented
- ☐ Visionary
- ☐ Win-Win Attitude
- ☐ Wisdom

© 2013 Unaltered Reproduction Rights Granted, Marketing Tao, LLC

The Ultimate Questions Book ~ Life

Blank Life Wheel

Directions: In the blank sections of the wheel add your top 8 Life Values / Qualities from the previous assessment. For each section, circle the number that represents your current level of satisfaction in that area. The higher the number, the greater your level of satisfaction.

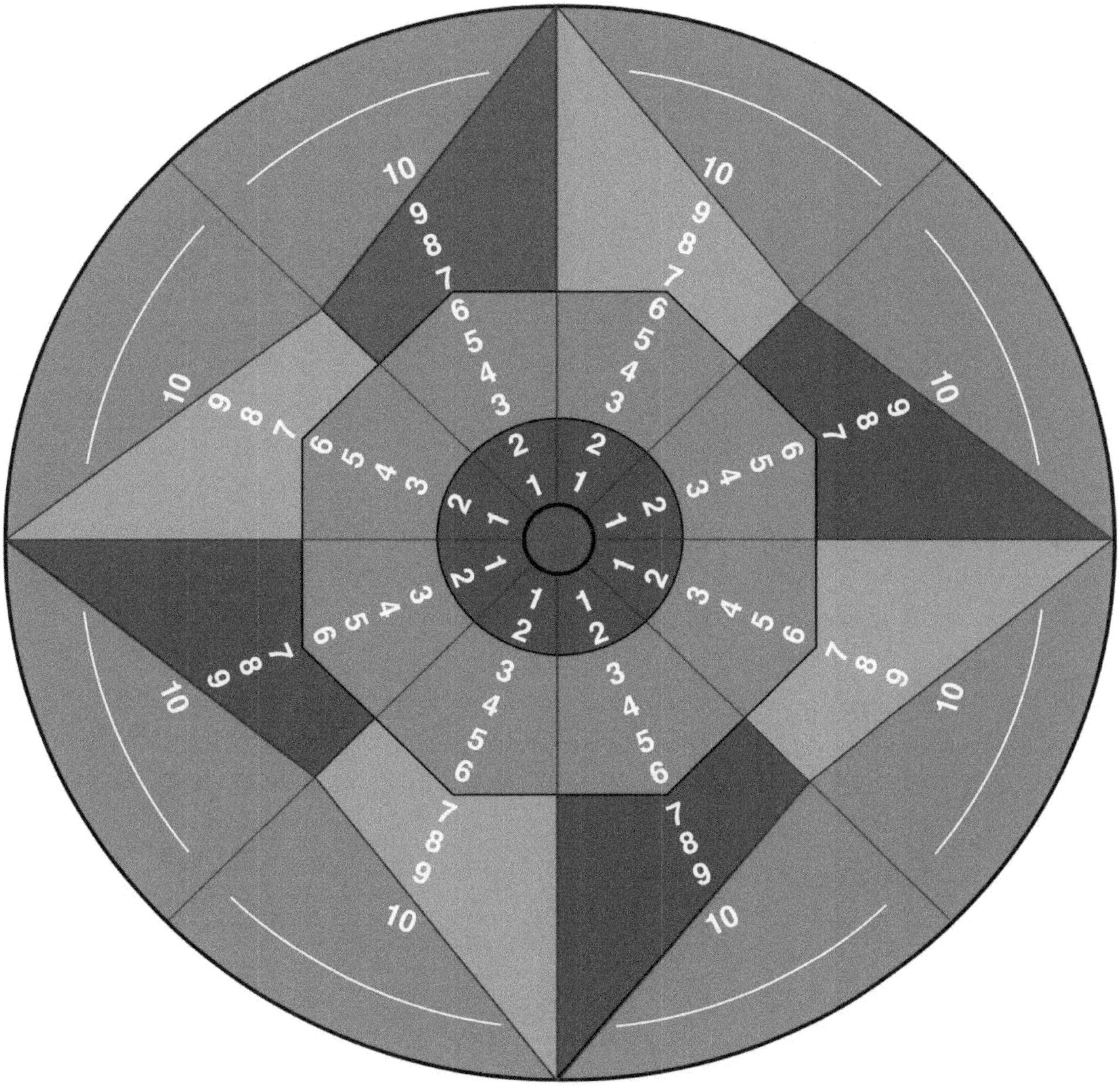

© 2013 Unaltered Reproduction Rights Granted, Marketing Tao, LLC

Life Quotes

If it is to be, it is up to me.
~ Anon

The last of human freedoms - the ability to choose one's attitude in a given set of circumstances.
~ Viktor Frankl

I was always looking outside myself for strength and confidence, but it comes from within. It was there all the time.
~ Anna Freud

The best way out of a problem is through it.
~ Anon

No pressure, no diamonds.
~ Mary Case

I don't want to be a passenger in my own life.
~ Diane Ackerman

Genius is an infinite capacity to take life by the scruff of the neck.
~ Katherine Hepburn

Everybody is talented, original, and has something important to say.
~ Brenda Ueland

It is brave to be involved.
~ Gwendolyn Brooks

The world belongs to the energetic.
~ Ralph Waldo Emerson

What really matters is what you do with what you have.
~ Shirley Lord

Trust your gut.
~ Barbara Walters

Try not to become a man of success, but rather a man of value.
~ Albert Einstein

Every man is the architect of his own fortune.
~ Sallust

Between stimulus and response there is a space. In that space is our power to choose our response. In our response lie our growth and our freedom.
~ Viktor Frankl

In times of change, learners inherit the Earth, while the learned find themselves beautifully equipped to deal with a world that no longer exists.
~ Eric Hoffer

I am a man of fixed and unbending principles, the first of which is to be flexible at all times.
~ Everett Dirksen

A community is like a ship; everyone ought to be prepared to take the helm.
~ Henrik Ibsen

Do not dwell in the past; do not dream of the future; concentrate the mind on the present moment.
~ Buddha

When one door closes, another opens; but we often look so long and so regretfully upon the closed door that we do not see the one that has opened for us.
~ Alexander Graham Bell

A life spent making mistakes is not only more honorable, but more useful than a life spent doing nothing.
~ George Bernard Shaw

Everything can be taken from a man or a woman but one thing: the last of human freedoms to choose one's attitude in any given set of circumstances, to choose one's own way.
~ Viktor Frankl

I have a simple philosophy: Fill what's empty. Empty what's full. Scratch where it itches.
~ Alice Roosevelt Longworth

I arise in the morning torn between a desire to improve the world and a desire to enjoy the world. This makes it hard to plan the day.
~ E.B. White

He who has a why to live can bear almost any how.
~ Friedrich Nietzsche

Don't let life discourage you; everyone who got where he is had to begin where he was.
~ Richard L. Evans

Don't go through life, grow through life.
~ Eric Butterworth

Seventy percent of success in life is showing up.
~ Woody Allen

Life isn't a matter of milestones, but of moments.
~ Rose Kennedy

May you live all the days of your life.
~ Jonathan Swift

Never be bullied into silence. Never allow yourself to be made a victim. Accept no one's definition of your life; define yourself.
~ Harvey Fierstein

Ever more people today have the means to live, but no meaning to live for.
~ Viktor Frankl

I cannot give you the formula for success, but I can give you the formula for failure: which is, Try to please everybody.
~ Herbert B. Swope

If I have seen farther than others, it is because I was standing on the shoulders of giants.
~ Isaac Newton

You must unite your constituents around a common cause and connect with them as human beings.
~ James Kouzes & Barry Posner

The price of greatness is responsibility.
~ Winston Churchill

My life is my message.
~ Mahatma Gandi

Nothing in life is to be feared, it is only to be understood. Now is the time to understand more, so that we may fear less.
~ Marie Curie

When we are no longer able to change a situation - we are challenged to change ourselves.
~ Viktor Frankl

Holding on to anger is like grasping a hot coal with the intent of throwing it at someone else; you are the one who gets burned.
~ Buddha

Beware the barrenness of a busy life.
~ Socrates

The Ultimate Questions Book ~ Life

S.M.A.R.T. Goals Checklist

Specific
- ☐ What precisely is expected?
- ☐ Be as specific as possible.
- ☐ What will you have when the specific task is complete?
- ☐ What will the outcome be?

Measurable
- ☐ How would you know you have achieved success?
- ☐ How many tasks do you need to do?
- ☐ For how long?
- ☐ Make it a tangible process.

Achievable
- ☐ Is this achievable?
- ☐ What would be achievable?
- ☐ Do you have the skills or resources necessary to meet this goal?

Reasonable
- ☐ Is this a reasonable goal?
- ☐ What might be the obstacles?
- ☐ Considering everything else you have going on, can you achieve this goal?

Time-Oriented
- ☐ When will you be done?
- ☐ When will your tasks be scheduled?
- ☐ How long will it take to accomplish each task?
- ☐ When is the ideal time for this goal to be completed?

© 2013 Unaltered Reproduction Rights Granted, Marketing Tao, LLC

About the Work

We live in a time of great change. Faced with some of the most difficult challenges our world has ever known, we feel an urgency to find solutions to make our lives better. We want answers and we want them now!

In general, we focus on **getting the right answer not on asking the right questions.** Why is this? Perhaps it stems from an innate curiosity and a desire to make sense of the world. Perhaps it comes from a fear of the unknown or the need for a quick fix. It may also result from the need for blind acceptance of some *truth* where any form of questioning is strongly discouraged or denied. Perhaps we think we already have the answer, so why ask any questions at all? Whatever the case, there is no doubt human beings like answers.

When we focus on "getting the right answers," rather than "asking the right questions," we limit ourselves. We move into dualistic thinking: "I either have the right answer or I don't." We think in terms of yes or no, right or wrong, good or bad. **This black and white framework enables only surface inquiry**, at best, and quells deeper investigation and the ability to engage with others in meaningful ways. We lose the opportunity to generate new solutions to old problems.

Why are asking the right questions important? Because they generate beneficial lasting change. Empowering questions make possible diverse perspectives, which in turn lead to sustainable solutions to complicated challenges. They enable people to engage in dynamic transformational conversations out of which new ideas are born.

To generate the type of change our world needs, **we must raise penetrative questions to challenge current assumptions**; assumptions that keep us disempowered to affect change. The key in creating a positive, empowering future is asking positive, empowering questions now! So, what are you waiting for?

About the Authors

Kathy Jo Slusher, PCC, ELI-MP, Founder of Marketing Tao, LLC, has dedicated her life to help service-based socially conscious business owners make their business a success through sharing their passion. She believes that when your intention is on your passion and helping others, money is a natural bi-product. *It's not what you sell but what you stand for that makes you a success.* She is deeply committed to helping soloprofessionals and small business owners implement mindful marketing techniques and strategies to attract their ideal clients while making a difference in the world.

Kathy Jo is a Co-Founder of The REAL Results Coaching Exchange, partner in Coaching Skills for Leaders, a member of the International Coach Federation, and Vice-President of the United Nations Association of the US, Indianapolis Chapter.

Denny Balish, PCC, ELI-MP, Professional Certified Coach and Founder of ThreeFold Life Coaching, has dedicated her life's work to the development of Human Potential. She believes that each person has within themselves the desire and ability to be a positive force for change in the world and, by sharing one's unique gifts and talents with others, global change is possible. Denny is deeply committed to helping people and organizations get and stay powerfully on-purpose so they can be the change they wish to see in the world. Denny is a member of the International Coach Federation (ICF), Association for Global New Thought (AGNT), and founding board member of Spirit's Light Foundation, an alternative youth and family ministry with the Association of Unity Churches International.

Other Valuable Resources

For Coaches, Consultants, and Service-Based Small Businesses

 **Ultimate Questions Books**

The real power in transformation is not in the answers, but in the questions we ask. If coaches, therapists or consultants are unsure of the questions to ask, client results are greatly impacted.

This series of books is specifically designed for coaches, consultants, therapists and others who are in a place where they need some fresh ideas to get themselves, a client, or anyone else unstuck. www.UltimateQuestionsBook.com

 **Marketing Made Practical**

Marketing Made Practical is a Home Study Program designed for those who are overwhelmed with all the options and don't have a handle on how to make the marketing process into an effective, successful strategy.

Marketing Made Practical is specifically designed for service-based soloprofessionals or small business owners who are just getting started or have a limited experience and need an organized approach to marketing. www.MarketingMadePractical.com

 **Marketing Strategies University**

Marketing Strategies University is an online training program that walks you through how to create a strong marketing and business development plan.

Marketing Strategies University cuts to the chase of marketing. We don't dive into the theory of marketing – but focus on practical steps to create and implement powerful marketing strategies.

This unique online training program is designed for service-based soloprofessionals or small business owners who have reached a certain level in their business where they are ready to create the systems and strategies for their marketing to take them to the next level of success. www.MarketingStrategiesUniversity.com

 **Marketing Strategies Success**

Marketing Strategies Success is an online membership forum which brings together motivation and information into a community of like-minded business owners all working to create change through their business.

Through topic specific open Q & A calls & recordings, to an interactive forum where members share ideas, to a mentoring component of Success Stories, where successful entrepreneurs share their success secrets, this group will help those who have a message to share through their business but need marketing know-how & structure to accomplish their mission. www.MarketingStrategiesSuccess.com

For Leadership Development Support

 **Coaching Skills for Leaders**

Employees don't leave companies, they leave managers.

According to the Gallup Poll, 71% of employees studied said they were either not engaged or actively disengaged at work. This employee disengagement results in $370 Billion lost annually. That's a huge amount.

In today's environment, talented individuals are arguably an organization's most valuable resource. Yet studies show, high potential employees have a higher turnover rate than any other employee population.

Leaders need to be flexible, adaptable, creative and resourceful to deal with the reality of our economic times. Coaching Skills for Leaders will take you

and your organization through The Coaching Clinic, a specialized training program where you acquire a new approach to old issues. This process offers a step-by-step process of a coaching conversation in how to conduct & lead those difficult conversations. You will learn how to address organizational challenges through a step-by-step structured approach to facilitate your own coaching conversation, and develop partners and accountability standards across the board. Thus you will be transforming managers into true Leaders. www.Coaching-Skills-for-Leaders.com

Lifestyle, Leadership, Legacy

What are you working for?

As a business owner or executive you've worked hard to get where you are at. But how has this helped the lifestyle you want to lead? If you're tired to living to work instead of working to live, this program is for you.

We will identify your desired lifestyle, look at how to improve your leadership ability so you can more effectively lead those around you as well as your own life and create a lasting legacy to leave behind.

On-Purpose Leadership Development

For on-purpose professionals who want to develop their leadership acumen while expanding their consciousness. This program formulates a plan of action to break through all obstacles limiting your success, while building powerful skills to help you lead with purpose, including: manage conflict and chaos with greater ease, use your intuition for effortless decision-making, communicate effectively and persuasively, maximize your ability to engage and influence people in positive ways, and feel empowered to affect change in yourself and others.

For Specialized Support for Non-Profits, Social Enterprises and Cultural Creatives

 **Life Purpose Coaching**

Empowering individuals in their midlife years to create a life of deeper meaning and purpose by not only connecting with their authentic voice and innate wisdom, but also by helping them aligning their skills, talents and interests with their desire to give back in meaningful ways.

 **On-Purpose Career Transition**

For individuals in all phases of career and job transition who seek to purposefully align their skills and abilities with their passion for a satisfying career; one that enables them to give back in meaningful ways. Make a living while making a difference! This program is customized to fit individual needs.

For More Information Contact:

Marketing Tao, LLC
Kathy Jo Slusher
Email   info@MarketingTao.com
Call   317.536.5544
Click   www.MarketingTao.com
Click   www.TheREALResultsCoachingExchange.com

Threefold Life
Denny Balish
Email   info@threefoldlife.com
Call   708.209.6977
Click   www.Threefoldlife.com